The Right Environment

Debra J. Housel, M.S. Ed.

Consultant

Michelle Alfonsi
Engineer, Southern California
Aerospace Industry

Image Credits: Cover & p.1 iStock; pp.15, 17, 19, 25 (illustrations) Tim Bradley; pp.4–8 (background), 12 (bottom), 14, 19 (background), 20 (left), 21 (right & background), 22–23, 25, 27 (background) iStock; pp.28–29 (illustration) Janelle Bell-Martin; p.23 (right bottom) Danté Fenolio/Science Source; pp.2–3 Dr. P. Marazzi/ Science Source; p.12 (top) Frans Lanting/MINT Images/Science Source; p.9 Hans Reinhard/ Science Source; p.6 John Serrao/Science Source; p.16 (right) Robert Francis/UIG/Science Source; all other images from Shutterstock.

Library of Congress Cataloging-in-Publication Data

Housel, Debra J., author.
  The right environment / Debra J. Housel ; consultants, Sally Creel, Ed.D. ; curriculum consultant, Leann Iacuone, M.A.T., NBCT, ATC Riverside Unified School District, Jill Tobin California Teacher of the Year Semi-Finalist Burbank Unified School District.
    pages cm
  Summary: "There's no place like home! But why is home so great? It's a place that meets your needs. You feel safe. The food is good. And you have somewhere to sleep. But what is good for you is very different than what camels or fish need. They need different things to survive and make their own home, sweet home!"— Provided by publisher.
  Audience: K to grade 3.
  Includes index.
  ISBN 978-1-4807-4641-1 (pbk.)
  ISBN 978-1-4807-5085-2 (ebook)
1. Ecology—Juvenile literature.
2. Biotic communities—Juvenile literature.
3. Adaptation (Biology)—Juvenile literature. I. Title.
QH541.14.H67 2015
577—dc23
                                        2014034263

Teacher Created Materials

5301 Oceanus Drive
Huntington Beach, CA 92649-1030
http://www.tcmpub.com

ISBN 978-1-4807-4641-1

Table of Contents

Home Sweet Home

It's a warm summer day. You go inside because you feel hot and sweaty. The air conditioning is on. It feels good! It keeps your house just the right temperature. Air conditioners and furnaces make it possible for humans to live almost anywhere. In fact, many of us spend much of our time inside.

But wild animals and plants live outside. These **organisms** must live in the right habitat, or home, to survive. Each habitat must have the right kind of weather, food, and land for those who live in it. Some plants and animals do better in wet places. Others do better in dry places. Some organisms prefer to live in places with a lot of insects. Others do best in places with few insects. There are many different types of habitats. The right **environment** allows plants and animals to do more than survive. It allows them to thrive.

As ostriches breathe in, moisture in their beaks evaporates, cooling them down.

Tree Frog

Tree frogs thrive in a wet environment, and the rainforest doesn't start with the word *rain* for no reason. It's the perfect home for this tree hopper.

Ecosystems

The plants and animals in habitats that are in the same area make up an **ecosystem**. Water, soil, sunlight, and other nonliving things are included in an ecosystem, too. Each ecosystem has different things in it. But they're all filled with life forms that rely on one another to survive.

Think of a meadow. Clover grows in a meadow. A rabbit eats the clover. An owl eats the rabbit. Later, the owl dies. Its body falls to the ground. Insects, worms, and other **decomposers** break it down. Soon, its body is gone. Some of the **nutrients** from the owl go back into the dirt for new clover to use. Worms also absorb some of the nutrients. Later, moles will eat the worms.

Every plant or animal has a niche, or role, to play in an ecosystem. Some living things may compete with one another for things that they need. Others may help one another survive.

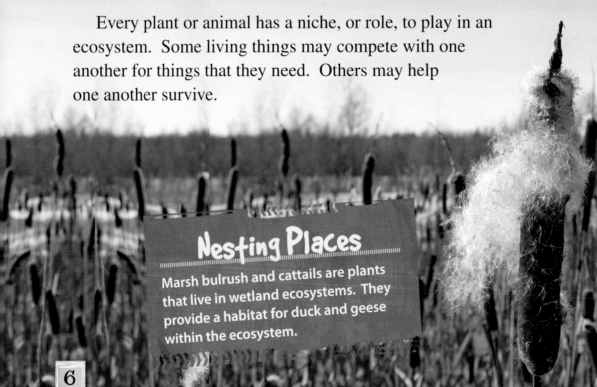

Nesting Places

Marsh bulrush and cattails are plants that live in wetland ecosystems. They provide a habitat for duck and geese within the ecosystem.

Starting from Scratch

Natural disasters, such as floods, fires, and volcanic eruptions, can change ecosystems in dramatic ways.

After a volcano created the island of Surtsey, scientists watched its ecosystem form.

Then, birds came to eat the bugs.

First, winds blew seeds onto the black rocks.

When these seeds sprouted, bugs came to eat the plants.

Finding Food

Food is an important part of any habitat or ecosystem. There must be enough of the right food for each animal living there. If there isn't enough food, animals will compete with one another for every meal. To stay alive, they may need to eat new foods. They can develop new skills. Or they may find a new home. Or else, they risk death.

Some animals eat only plants. They are **herbivores**. These animals do best in places with a large supply of their favorite plants.

Some animals eat other animals. These are **carnivores**. Their habitat must have enough of the right kinds of animals. The cheetah lives on the grasslands of Africa. It hunts wildebeests and gazelles. Lions are also carnivores. They compete with cheetahs for food. This means there must be a lot of gazelles and wildebeests and only a few cheetahs and lions. If there are too many carnivores, some will starve. This is because there will not be enough food for all the living things in the area.

A cheetah is a carnivore that can spot its prey up to three miles away!

Some animals eat both plants and animals. They are **omnivores**. Their habitats must have enough of the right kinds of plants and animals. A skunk is an omnivore. It eats roots, berries, bugs, worms, and frogs. Animals that eat a wider variety of plants and animals have an easier time finding food. And they have an easier time surviving.

Picky Eaters

The giant panda only eats one thing— bamboo. But bamboo is hard to grow. No one knows what causes bamboo to flower. And it can take 120 years to do so! To make matters worse, all the bamboo plants in a forest flower at once. After that, there is no food for giant pandas until new bamboo shoots poke out of the ground. This is one reason pandas are in danger.

Food Chains

A food chain shows how energy moves through an ecosystem. All food chains start with the sun. Sunlight provides the energy plants need to make their food. For example, grass is a plant that gets energy from the sun. Then, rabbits eat the grass. This gives rabbits energy to grow and produce more rabbits. Foxes eat the rabbits. This gives foxes energy to grow and produce more foxes. The chain continues with larger **predators** such as eagles. They get energy by eating the foxes.

Any change in a food chain can cause big problems. If there are too many predators, like eagles and foxes, it can be difficult for the predators to survive. They are competing for a limited number of rabbits. If the number of rabbits gets too low, there won't be enough food to support the predators. If plants stop growing, it can hurt the entire food chain! The fewer plants and animals there are in a food chain, the more fragile it is.

Keystone Species

A keystone species is a plant or an animal that has a strong effect on its ecosystem. The jaguar is a keystone species in the tropical rainforests of South America. It eats over 80 different kinds of animals. This keeps the number of all the other animals in check.

Food Webs

Most ecosystems have many food chains. Herbivores eat many different plants. Carnivores eat many different animals. Omnivores eat both. Multiple food chains overlap to create a complex food web.

energy

energy

energy

energy

energy

energy

energy

energy

energy

energy

Weathering the Seasons

Some ecosystems have warm **climates**. They may be hot and humid most days of the year. Other ecosystems have cold climates. They may usually be wet and rainy. But climates can change, too. Many places around the world have four seasons. In these places, trees may lose their leaves when it gets cold. Flowers may not bloom until spring. When the days grow short, some birds and insects fly south. They may spend their winter in warmer places.

Some animals don't leave when seasons change. Owls, squirrels, and wolves find food and places to stay warm throughout the winter. Other animals hibernate, or sleep, all winter long. Animals that hibernate start by eating a lot. A black bear can gain 30 pounds per week before climbing into its den to hibernate! Then, its heart and lungs slow down. The bear's body uses stored fat to stay alive through the winter months.

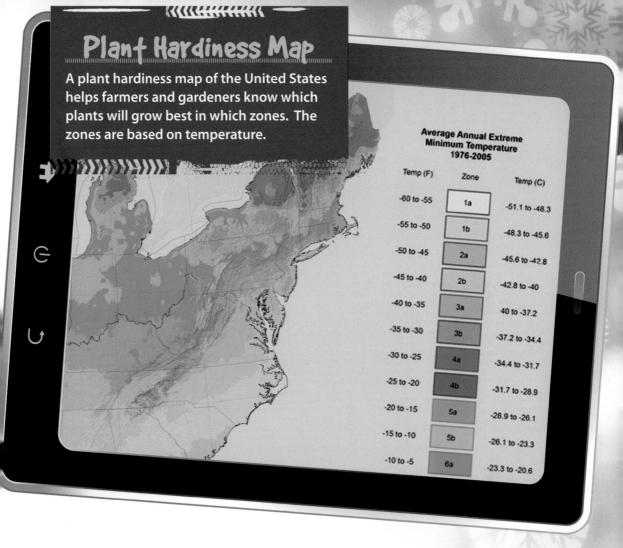

Plant Hardiness Map

A plant hardiness map of the United States helps farmers and gardeners know which plants will grow best in which zones. The zones are based on temperature.

Average Annual Extreme Minimum Temperature 1976-2005

Temp (F)	Zone	Temp (C)
-60 to -55	1a	-51.1 to -48.3
-55 to -50	1b	-48.3 to -45.6
-50 to -45	2a	-45.6 to -42.8
-45 to -40	2b	-42.8 to -40
-40 to -35	3a	40 to -37.2
-35 to -30	3b	-37.2 to -34.4
-30 to -25	4a	-34.4 to -31.7
-25 to -20	4b	-31.7 to -28.9
-20 to -15	5a	-28.9 to -26.1
-15 to -10	5b	-26.1 to -23.3
-10 to -5	6a	-23.3 to -20.6

In the desert, some animals sleep through the hottest part of the year. They **estivate** (ES-tuh-veyt). North American desert tortoises spend most of the year asleep in rock crevices or deep burrows. They only come out to eat or to find a mate.

No matter what the season is, temperature is an important part of any ecosystem. If the temperature changes, the perfect environment may no longer feel so perfect. Some organisms may find new ways to survive. They might shed their fur. They may find ways to build a warm nest. Others may need to find a new home. Some may even die.

Land Biomes

A biome is a large area that contains many ecosystems. Many biomes are named for the type of plants they have in them. Some land biomes have a lot of trees. Some have barely any. Other biomes are named for the climate of the area in which they are found. Some biomes are hot and dry. Some are cool and damp. The animals and plants that live in one biome might not be able to survive somewhere else.

The praying mantis lives in land biomes that have lots of green plants to hide among.

Levels of Organization

Scientists study organisms and their environments on many levels.

An ecosystem is made up of all the plants, animals, and nonliving things in that area.

A biome is a large area with many ecosystems in it.

An organism is one living thing.

A population is a group of species of organisms living in an area.

A community is a group of living things in the area.

The taiga (TAHY-guh), or pine forest, is the world's largest land biome. It covers the greatest percentage of Earth's landmasses.

Desert Biome

The desert biome is an extreme environment. It's very dry. Years may pass without any rainfall. It is usually quite hot. It may be 50° Celsius (120° Fahrenheit) during the day and then drop to 0°C (32°F) at night. The animals and plants that live there have found ways to survive in these harsh conditions.

Pebble plants live in the desert. But it's easy to miss them when they aren't in bloom. When rain falls, their small, wide leaves swell with water. The rest of the time, they blend in with the rocks. That way, thirsty animals won't eat them.

The fennec is a tiny fox that lives in the African desert. It digs a deep burrow and spends its days underground. Then, it comes out at night to hunt for small **mammals** and birds. The fennec fox has huge ears. They let heat escape from its body. The ears also help the fox hear and track its prey in the dark desert.

fennec fox

In parts of the Atacama Desert in Chile, it hasn't rained for centuries!

Biome Breakdown

How many biomes are there? It depends who you ask. Some people say there are five major biomes: aquatic, desert, forest, grassland, and tundra. But some break them down into more categories.

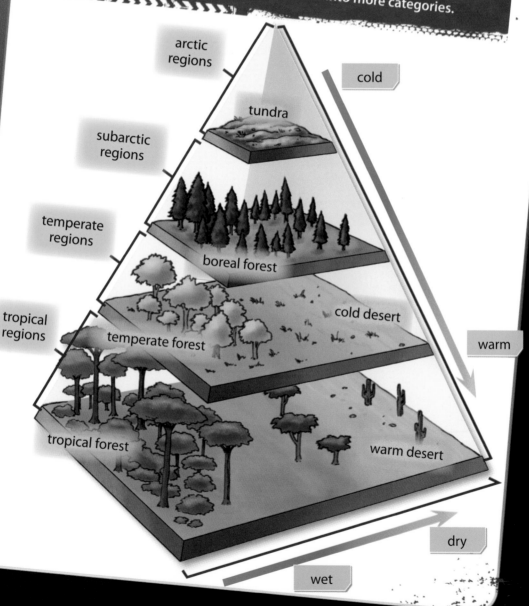

arctic regions

cold

tundra

subarctic regions

temperate regions

boreal forest

cold desert

tropical regions

temperate forest

warm

tropical forest

warm desert

dry

wet

Tundra Biome

Another kind of fox lives on the tundra. It lives in a burrow for a different reason. It must survive the extreme cold of the Arctic winter. The tundra is cold and windy. Temperatures can drop to -70°C (-44°F)! The Arctic fox's ears are small, and its muzzle is short. This keeps it from losing heat.

The Arctic fox's fur changes color with the seasons. Its fur is white during the winter and brown in the summer. This helps the fox blend in with its environment. The fox catches voles, or small rodents, that run in tunnels under the snow. The fox also follows polar bears from a distance. When the bear kills a walrus, it only eats the blubber. Then, the fox eats what is left.

The tundra's growing season is short. Winter is long and the dirt is always frozen. No trees can grow there. But grass, moss, and Arctic poppies cover the ground. These plants have short roots and can withstand the cold.

Arctic fox

The Arctic tundra is the world's youngest biome. It formed just 10,000 years ago.

The Cold Hard Truth

An elephant would have a hard time surviving in the Arctic. But about 20,000 years ago, a relative of the elephant did just that. The woolly mammoth is an ancient relative of today's elephants. It lived over 20,000 years ago during a very cold time in our planet's history.

Elephants' large ears keep them cool in the heat.

Mammoths' ears were much smaller.

Elephants use their trunks for drinking and showering. But that gets tricky when all the water is frozen.

A thick coat of fur and an extra layer of fat on a mammoth's back kept it warm.

19

Tracking Biomes

As the climate changes, biomes may move. Thousands of years ago, parts of Africa were green and wet. Now, there is a large desert in Africa. Scientists predict that by 2100, 40 percent of biomes will change.

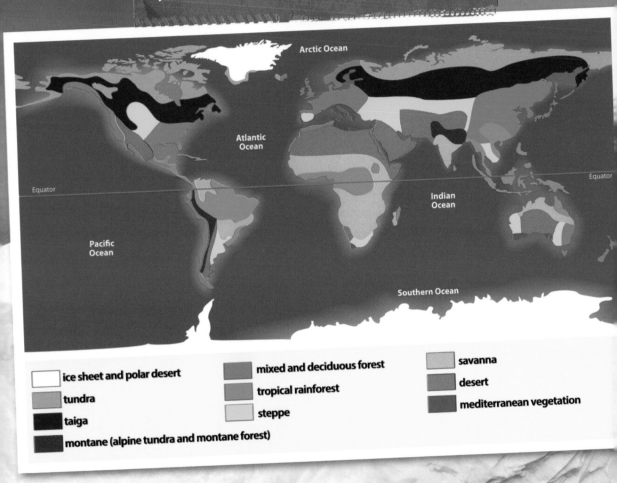

ice sheet and polar desert

tundra

taiga

montane (alpine tundra and montane forest)

mixed and deciduous forest

tropical rainforest

steppe

savanna

desert

mediterranean vegetation

Water Biomes

Earth is covered in water. There are oceans, rivers, ponds, swamps, and lakes. Water can also be found in icy glaciers and underground. Water biomes are home to some of the most amazing plants and animals on Earth. Everything from shrimp to sharks call water their home.

Room to Grow

The ocean is home to some of the world's largest animals, including whales. And with over 70 percent of Earth covered in water, even plants find ways to stretch and grow. Kelp is the fastest-growing organism in the world. It can grow up to two feet a day!

Saltwater Biomes

Saltwater biomes are the largest biomes on Earth. Ninety-seven percent of the world's water is in the oceans. Oceans are saltwater. The organisms living in saltwater cannot live in freshwater. Some organisms live in the shallow area of the ocean. Different animals live in the deep parts of the ocean. Most of the ocean is too deep for sunlight to reach plants.

Coral Reefs

Coral reefs form in warm, clear, shallow ocean water. Coral are tiny animals. They absorb nutrients from the water and make a rock-hard shell. Coral reefs are important ecosystems. They are home to fish, sharks, dolphins, and more.

Oceans don't have seasons. But there are changes in the ocean's water temperature and the amount of sunlight received. Some ocean animals **migrate**. They may migrate to warmer water to give birth and breed. Then they migrate back to colder waters to feed. California gray whales do this. They give birth during the winter off the coast of Mexico and they spend summer off the coast of Alaska. Other ocean animals stay in one area their whole lives. Their habitats meet their needs year round.

A Light in the Dark

Some animals have found amazing ways to survive. Flashlight fish have lights below their eyes to help them find food. When they want to hide, skin flaps cover their lights.

Freshwater Biomes

Freshwater biomes can be found in moving waters such as streams and rivers. Or they can be found in still waters such as lakes, ponds, and swamps. Less wildlife lives in moving water than in still water. And the deeper and faster the water is, the fewer organisms live there. These biomes are found on every continent except Antarctica. All the water there is ice.

Estuaries

Estuary (ES-choo-er-ee) biomes are places where saltwater and freshwater mix. This happens where freshwater comes down river and flows into an ocean or sea. Each day, as the tide rises, saltwater flows into estuaries. Many ocean fish lay their eggs here.

The plants that live in estuaries have found ways to absorb and store salt safely.

Thirsty?

Just under three percent of all the water on Earth is freshwater! That means freshwater organisms must compete for food and space. Saltwater plants and animals have more options.

A Closer Look

If you glance at a pond, it may seem as if nothing is happening. Ponds have very still water. They don't have tides or currents. But if you watch all day, you will see that ponds are busy places.

A water snake slithers across the pond's surface. It avoids the heron and searches for the frog.

A heron eyes the water snake.

Tadpoles eat the green algae (AL-jee) floating on the surface.

A box turtle suns itself on a log.

A bullfrog croaks noisily.

Room for Everyone

Earth's creatures have found ways to survive in amazing places. Bacteria grow in volcanoes where temperatures reach 56°C (133°F). Tigers hunt in the mountains of Russia where the air is thin and cold. Camels can drink up to 76 liters (20 gallons) of water in one sitting. This allows them to wander for weeks in the desert without water. Each of these creatures has found the right environment for them. If their environment changes, they will need to change, too. If they don't, they will be in danger of dying.

Like other creatures, humans thrive in environments that are rich with life. We have found ways to live in extreme places. We've made most of the planet our home! But not all life forms are as flexible. We can help those life forms by protecting our planet. We can improve the quality of our air, soil, and water. We can leave space for plants and animals. Taking these steps will create a world in which millions of different creatures can flourish and grow.

bacteria under a microscope

Balancing the Equation

Plants and animals can't do math the way we can. But in their own way, they each make important calculations. Finding the right environment means balancing many things. When all these elements add up, they create just the right environment.

THE RIGHT ENVIRONMENT

Think Like a Scientist

Do lima beans prefer a sunny or shady habitat? Experiment and find out!

What to Get

- 1 two-liter clear bottle
- 1 two-liter green bottle
- 2 one-gallon sandwich bags
- 6 lima bean seeds
- pebbles
- potting soil
- water

What to Do

1 Have an adult help you cut the top from each bottle. Recycle the bottle tops.

2 Pour pebbles in the bottom of each bottle. Pour three inches of potting soil over the pebbles. Press three seeds into the soil of each bottle. Cover the seeds with soil.

3 Gently pour $\frac{2}{3}$ cup water into each bottle.

4 Cover each bottle with a sandwich bag. Place one bottle in a sunny window and one bottle in the shade.

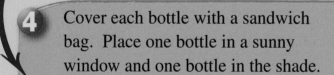

5 For two weeks, record daily what happens inside each habitat. Compare the results.

Glossary

carnivores—animals that eat meat

climates—usual types of weather places get

decomposers—living things that feed on and break down dead plants or animals

ecosystem—everything that exists in a particular environment

environment—the natural world

estivate—to pass the summer in an inactive or resting state

herbivores—animals that only eat plants

mammals—types of animals that feed milk to their young and are usually covered in hair or fur

migrate—to move from one area to another at different times of the year

nutrients—substances that living things need to grow

omnivores—animals that eat both plants and animals

organisms—living things

predators—animals that live by killing and eating other animals

Index

Your Turn!

The World Outside Your Door

Make a list of the wild animals and plants that live in your area. Think about how the plants and animals have adapted to the environment. Discuss with a family member whether there is a keystone species. Imagine what might happen to the ecosystem if that keystone species were removed.